## Craig Conley

Prof. ODD FELLOW's
Forgotten Wisdom

For Ken,
with deep
affection.
Craig

Dedicated to
"His Grace the Dook of
Ampassy-Etcetera."*

* *All the Year Round,* Sept. 22, 1866

The sign **&** is said to be properly called Emperor's hand, from having been first invented by some imperial personage, but by whom deponent saith not.

◆————William Shepard Walsh, *Handy-book of Literary Curiosities* (1892)

Brnie Yuman, longtime manager of magicians Siegfried & Roy, called himself the duo's "**AMPERSAND**" (Jim Mydlach, *The Secret Life of Siegfried and Roy*, 2008).

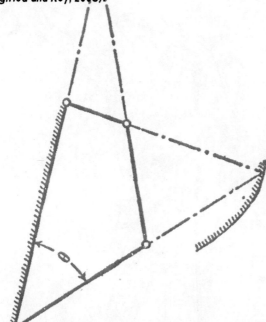

The word "ampersand" has no perfect rhymes. However, "**AMPERSAND** rimes with damper hand" (John Baker Opdycke, *Don't Say It: A Cyclopedia of English Use and Abuse*, 1939).

**AMPERSAND** makes a good pet name. The poet Edwin Arlington Robinson describes a cat named Ampersand who "talks ugly" and is "shaped like '&'" (Robert L. Gale, *An Edwin Arlington Robinson Encyclopedia*, 2006). In the comic book series *Y: The Last Man*, by Brian K. Vaughan and Pia Guerra, a Capuchine monkey called Ampersand is a companion to hero Yorick Brown. And Ampersand is the name of a prize-winning racehorse in Ferdinand Mount's *The Man Who Rode Ampersand* (2002).

# Is the Ampersand a Punctuation Mark?

Left
Bracket

Right
Parenthesis

Comma

Left Single
Quotation Mark

Hereafter is the sign, the ampersand
Between this present and the time to come.
—————————Samuel French Morse, *The Changes*, 1964

TYCOOON & WIFE the caption said.
The smirk was in the ampersand.
————◆————Ward S. Just, *Echo House*, 1998


A boastful ampersand.
————◆————Ian Patterson, "Laugh Like a Piano,"
*Time to Get Here*, 2003

The ampersand was originally called 'and-pussy-and' because its shape suggests a pussy-cat sitting up and raising its forepaw.

————◆————Edward Walford, *The Antiquary*, Vol. 32, 1896

My graceful, swanlike ampersand!

———◆———Carolyn Wells, *A Whimsey Anthology*, 1906

When I've a pen in a listless hand, I'm always making an Amperzand!
———◆———*Punch*, April 17, 1869

Can you find 8 ampersands hidden in this gentleman's portrait?

Of all the types in a printer's hand
Commend me to the ampersand,
For he's the gentleman (seems to me)
Of the typographical companie.

————◆————Carolyn Wells, *A Whimsey Anthology*, 1906

In his poem "Meditation Celestial & Terrestrial," Wallace Stevens links heaven and earth with an ampersand.

For such a concise symbol, "ampersand" has triple the letters and syllables as the word it stands for. (Robertson Cochrane, *Wordplay: Origins, Meanings, and Usage of the English Language*, 1996.) "Ampersand cleverly divides into three words with a progressive number of letters ————► **AM PER SAND**" (Richard Lederer, *The Word Circus*, 1997).

In a science fiction story, a "telepath sees people's thoughts as run-on sentences connected by **AMPERSAND** characters" (William Barton, "Off on a Starship," *The Year's Best Science Fiction*, 2004).

**&,** humble **AMPERSAND**, reminds us all
Of something more, of things about to be.
(It spells Eternity !)
—Charles Ballard, *Poet Lore*, 1947

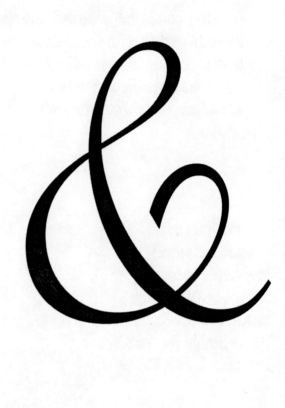

Is the ampersand a symbol of the Gordian Knot of lore?

Legend tells us that Gordius, king of Gordium, tied a knot so intricately tangled that the ends of its cord were imperceptible. He prophesied that whoever untied the knot would rule all of Asia. Alexander the Great is said to have boldly sliced the Gordian Knot with his sword. Today, the phrase "cut the Gordian knot" means to solve a problem by a decisive measure, à la Alexander.

"The ampersand ... is the Gordian knot, or Whitman's 'old knot of contrariety' or the untied naught, the 'CIPHER' we might still make of ourselves."
——◆—Stephen Yenser, *The Consuming Myth*, 1987

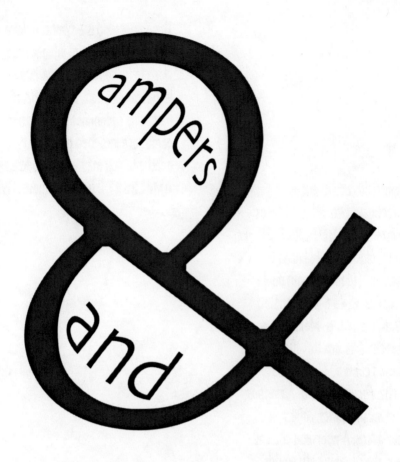

In *Soul Searching*, the poet Dennis Cooley writes ampersand as two words, with and hanging directly below *ampers*, thusly:

ampers
and

Cooley's notation suggests the two sections of the ampersand symbol.

The ampersand is a symbol of love ————◆————of intimacy too close to be separated by a three-letter conjunction. Indeed, *Handicraft* magazine recommends that when names are inscribed on a heart pendant, "you may want to add an **AMPERSAND** between them" (1974).

Ampersands and hyphens characterize two different types of citizens. An "**AMPERSAND** citizen" (such as a "Mexican **&** American") identifies with dual ethnicities, while a "Hyphenated citizen" (such as a "Mexican-American") assimilates the adopted culture. (Jeffrey D. Schultz, *Encyclopedia of Minorities in American Politics,* 2000.) In other words, Ampersand citizens "keep their feet in both worlds" (Samuel P. Huntington, *Who Are We?,* 2004). Speaking of national origin, the ampersand celebrates a Roman heritage: Cicero's secretary Marcus Tullius Tiro is credited with inventing the ampersand c. 63 BC as part of an extensive shorthand system (approximately 5,000 signs).

To "read every **AMPERSAND**" is to carefully scrutinize a document, as in the poetry of B. Koppany (*Collected Poems, 1971-2000*).

Wordsmith James Nelson Hulme likens the ampersand to an Archon, one of the nine chief magistrates in Ancient Athens (*Alliteration*, 1882).

The ampersand (bottom left) is often used in place of the G clef (top left) in the musical notation of folk ballads (W. Edson Richmond, *The Journal of American Folklore*, Vol. 69, No. 274, Oct. - Dec., 1956).

# ESPIRITU SANTO

Ampersand is as endless as tropic sea shore.

————◆————D. H. Francis, "X-Terminated Words," *Word Ways:
The Journal of Recreational Linguistics,* 1975

During World War II, "Ampersand" was a code name for Espiritu Santo Island
(now known as Vanuatu), in the New Hebrides Islands (Frederick G. Ruffner,
*Code Names Dictionary,* 1963). Espiritu Santo Island was the inspiration for
James A. Michener's famous novel *Tales of the South Pacific.*

Graced with a pretzeled, sinuous ampersand.
———◆———Anthony Hecht, *Collected Earlier Poems*, 1990

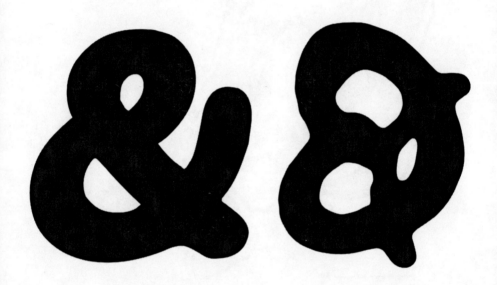

The poet Erica Hunt speaks of a tongue-tied person with a pretzel-like ampersand caught in the throat ("Poem for a Second," *Gathering Ground*, 2006).

Some scalawags make a point of always speaking the &'s full name. For example, word maven William Safire pronounces the department store "Lord & Taylor" as "Lord ampersand Taylor" ("On Language," *New York Times*, July 9, 1989). Name expert Leslie Dunkling suggests that pronouncing the ampersand is correct: "I once visited a shop which displayed its name as &. This symbol should be verbalised as AMPERSAND" (*The Guiness Book of Names: Facts and Feats*, 1983).

Model railroad builders bend coat hangers into AMPERSANDS to grip a model while airbrushing paint (Robert Schleicher, *101 Projects for Your Model Railroad*, 2002).

Language expert Karlen Evins calls the AMPERSAND a "do-jiggy" (*I Didn't Know That*, 2007). That epithet is perhaps kinder than "thingumabob" and certainly more precise than "whatchamacallit."

The novelist Vladimir Nabokov used an ampersand to quantify the gap between humans and animals. "The difference between an ape's memory and a human memory is the difference between an ampersand and the British Museum library" (BBC interview, 1969).

An ampersand recalls figure skating:
"Ohioans skating ampersands beneath winter maples."
————◆————University of Tulsa, *Nimrod,* 1996

Billiards champion Semih Sayginer has a shot he calls "The Ampersand." Here's how one sports reporter described it: "With every last ounce of power he could muster, Semih stunned the audience one final time as he made his cue ball trace a line that resembled a giant ten-foot typewriter symbol on the table ————◆———— a masse shot he called 'The Ampersand.' As the point scored, the entire audience leapt to their feet and delivered to him a roaring standing ovation" (Ira Lee, "Sayginer, Massey and Yow Shine Brightly on ESPN 3-Cushion Grandmaster," May 24, 2007).

A manual for typographers published in 1917 acknowledged that there are many beautiful forms of the ampersand, yet it forbade their use in "ordinary book work" (Frank Souder Henry, *Printing for School and Shop*, 1917). Extraordinary books are another matter, however. An Italian manuscript from 1600 features no fewer than 14 extravagantly executed **AMPERSANDS** of five sorts on a single page.

This index card, this slender rubber band
Which always forms, when dropped, an
**AMPERSAND**.
—Vladimir Nabokov, *Pale Fire*, 1989

An **AMPERSAND** is considered a "fudge factor" in a palindrome. For example, "Lewd did I live & evil did I dwel" would not read the same backwards if the ampersand were spelled out as "and." (Richard Lederer, *Word Wizard*, 2006.) However, a semicolon could replace the ampersand in this instance.

An ampersand has two feet, at least in terms of prosody. Each stressed syllable (ámper) and (sánd) constitutes one metrical foot of poetry.

AMPERSAND the ewe, mare, cock and drake, rose caterpillar and cheese.
———◆———James Reaney, *Poems,* 1972

The ampersand awakens the hieroglyphic ancestry of the alphabet. The ampersand "pushes the language further in the direction of pure graphism, reminding us that Z, as a grapheme, is a pictogram of 'swan,' just as the O's are pictograms of 'eggs'" (Clive Scott, *The Spoken Image*, 1999).

Ampersands apparently "functioned as guides to devotion" in late medieval religious texts (John C. Hirsh, *The Boundaries of Faith*, 1996).

The English novelist William Gerhardie (1895-1977) "adopted the **AMPERSAND** as his personal cipher: 'on symbolical, mystical grounds.'"
—Dido Davies, *William Gerhardie: A Biography* (1990)

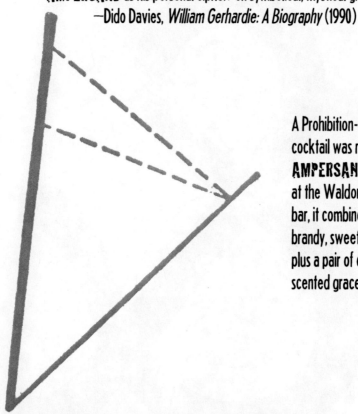

A Prohibition-era cocktail was named the **AMPERSAND**. Served at the Waldorf-Astoria bar, it combined "gin, brandy, sweet vermouth, plus a pair of orange-scented grace notes."

The **AMPERSAND** is a teetotaler. In his tour de force entitled *Alliteration* (containing over 2,000 words, all beginning with the letter A), wordsmith James Nelson Hulme describes an ampersand addressing an anti-alcohol assembly: "And Ampersand, affably accepting appointment as affirmed, and attired accordingly, advanced affront Assembly, assumed authority, artly addressed all assembled, accredited all as able abstinence Advocates and avised adunanimous action and address—affabrous, appropriate and accrescent—against Alcohol and all alcoholic admixions; and Alcohol's admixers, and assotted admirers and abusers." (Hulme makes sure to define all his rare vocabulary words in footnotes!)

The ampersand is a symbol for pregnancy, as its shape resembles a woman with a swollen belly. For example, in Catherine Petroski's *A Bride's Passage*, a diarist begins using an ampersand as a codeword for her pregnancy: "In her diary Susan never breathes a word of sexual activity ... [but instead] has put a tiny, encrypted record of her reproductive life ————◆————fastidiously inked in nonwords ... her ampersand glyphs" (1997). Also: "When she looks at the desk she sees the ampersand key on the upper row of the typewriter keyboard, the **&** above the 7. It's shaped like herself" (Charles Baxter, *Believers*, 1997).

As insignificant as a wandering ampersand.

———◆———Ken W. Reardon, "Teamwork," 2004

Which came first: Ampersand Stream, or Lake, or Mountain? Here's an intriguing explanation from *The Gentleman's Magazine*, 1892:

"Ampersand is a mountain. It is a lake. It is a stream. The mountain stands in the heart of the Adirondack country, just near enough to the thoroughfare of travel for thousands of people to see it every year, and just far enough away from the beaten track to be unvisited, except by a very few of the wise ones who love to digress. Behind the mountain is the lake, which no lazy man has ever seen. Out of the lake flows the stream, winding down a long, untrodden forest valley, until at length it joins the Stony Creek waters, and empties into the Raquette River. Which of the three Ampersands has the prior claim to the name I cannot tell.

"Philosophically speaking, the mountain ought to be regarded as the father of the family, because it was undoubtedly there before the others existed. And the lake was probably the next on the ground, because the stream is its child. But man is not strictly correct in his nomenclature; and I conjecture that the little river, the last-born of the three, was the first to be called Ampersand, and then gave its name to its parent and grandparent. It is such a crooked stream, so bent and curved and twisted upon itself, so fond of turning around unexpected corners, and sweeping away in great circles from its direct course, that its first explorers christened it after the eccentric supernumerary of the alphabet which appears in the old spelling book as **&**."

The ampersand's history would appear to be relatively brief, at least in terms of page count. Jan Tschichold's *The Ampersand: Its Origin and Development* (1957) is only 24 pages. Melvin M. Miller's *The Origin and Historical Development of the Ampersand* (1965) is even shorter, at 15 pages. Lawrence C. Wroth's *Mystical Reflections on the* AMPERSAND (1937) is a mere 12 pages.

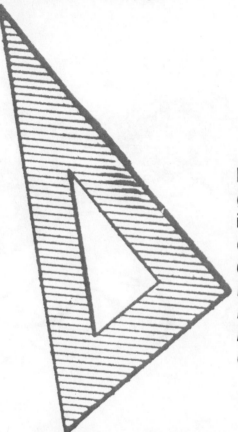

Humorist Lewis Grizzard recalls getting his shirt collar caught in a typewriter, narrowly escaping getting "typed to death by an out-of-control AMPERSAND" (*When My Love Returns from the Ladies Room, Will I Be Too Old to Care?*, 1987).

The AMPERSAND is "the single feature most useful to examine first when looking for writers' handwriting idiosyncrasies, or when comparing two examples of writing to check whether they are in the same hand" (Peter Beal, *A Dictionary of English Manuscript Terminology*, 2008).

Ripples of water where you were swimming,
Your questioning voice saying "Ampersand?"

———◆———Ruth Klüger, "Halloween and a Ghost," *Still Alive*, 2001

Ampersand, quicksand: what's the difference?

———◆———African-American minstrel Bert Williams,
qtd. in *Racechanges* by Susan Gubar, 2000

The ampersand is multilingual. "The ampersand logogram means the same whether it is being read by someone whose mother tongue is English, French, German, or indeed any other language whose writing system makes use of the ampersand" (James Essinger, *Spellbound: The Surprising Origins and Astonishing Secrets of English Spelling*, 2007). Indeed, linguist Alfred Charles Moorhouse tells us that "the AMPERSAND is used with the sense 'and' in several hundred languages" (*The Triumph of the Alphabet*, 1953).

Would-be calligraphers take note: "People who do not wish to paint or draw an AMPERSAND should not attempt lettering" (Jan Tschichold, *Treasury Of Alphabets And Lettering*, 1995).

The AMPERSAND has a good sense of humor. Indeed, Walter Kerr wrote in *Tragedy and Comedy* that "The sign of the ampersand always suggests comedy" (qtd. in *The Theatre of Friedrich Dürrenmatt* by Kenneth Whitton, 1980).

And the sign for a wheelchair
is exactly like an ampersand.
An ampersand.  An ampersand.
————◆————Craig Raine, *History*, 1994

People who don't know an ampersand from a hole in the ground.
———◆—Michael Beirut, *Looking Closer*, 1994

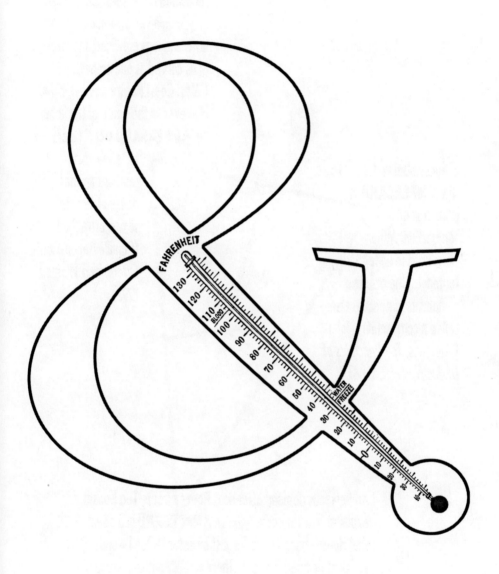

Nobel Laureate Derek Walcott's epic poem "Omeros"
features an ampersand-shaped rectal thermometer in Hell.

The curvaceous ampersand is renowned for its sensuality. "I can only imagine an afternoon with our arms and legs entwined, the two of us curved as one ampersand" (West Coast Poetry Review, 1974). However, in the genre of fan fiction, an "AMPERSAND story" refers to "a friendship relationship that does not include sexual attraction" (Camille Bacon-Smith, *Enterprising Women*, 1992).

In the symbol system of Logic, "the AMPERSAND '&' is the sign of conjunction. When '&' is used to unite two sentences, the resulting compound sentence is also called a conjunction" (John T. Kearnes, *The Principles of Deductive Logic*, 1988).

Ampersands demand attention. Poet Laureate Ted Kooser explains: "I never come upon an AMPERSAND in a poem that doesn't hang me up for just an instant while I wonder why the poet decided to use it. There is really nothing wrong with the word 'and,' and it doesn't attract any attention, but every ampersand requires a reader to think about it, if only for a second" (*The Poetry Home Repair Manual*, 2007).

# Etcephalon

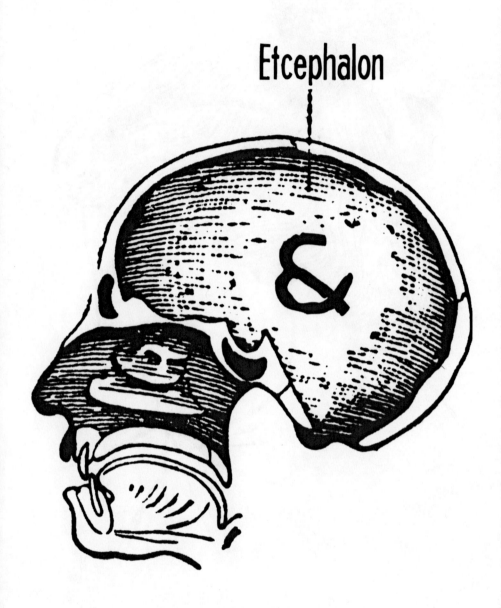

Who would ever think about the ampersand,
that odd symbol that is also a word.
———◆———Ulla E. Dydo, *A Stein Reader,* 1993

The hair had assumed an odd configuration, a flourishing curvilinear form with a large loop below and a smaller one above. "An ampersand," Eber mumbled.

————◆——Virgil Burnett, "The Golden Ampersand," *Descant*, 2005

Anglo-Saxon poets casually incorporated pagan runes into their manuscripts "just as a modern writer might use an ampersand with no consciousness of its being a compressed form of the Latin word et."

————◆————Robert DiNapoli, "Odd Characters: Runes in Old English Poetry," *Verbal Encounters*, 2005

"Any by itself plus itself with itself" is how the poet E. E. Cummings defined his ampersand. Cummings' sign was a "beautiful if somewhat self-centered, gigantic filiform **AMPERSAND**" (Lloyd N. Dendinger, *E. E. Cummings, the Critical Reception*, 1979). Cummings titled one of his books **&**.

In a science fiction story, a "telepath sees people's thoughts as run-on sentences connected by **AMPERSAND** characters" (William Barton, "Off on a Starship," *The Year's Best Science Fiction*, 2004).

In Ralph Waldo Emerson's Sermon XCVI, "Thy Will Be Done," an **AMPERSAND** is obscured by red sealing wax.
—*The Complete Sermons of Ralph Waldo Emerson, Vol. 3*, edited by Ronald A. Bosco (1992)

**&** as bone calcifies
leave this trace

————◆————Sydney Bernard Smith, "Poem Commencing
with an Ampersand," *The Book of Shannow*, 2007

Have you ever heard of an ampersand "catching
some Z's"? Knotted by tension, the sign is afflicted
by insomnia. Going without rest is much easier
than "sleeping bent into an ampersand" (Fitz Hugh
Ludlow, *The Heart of the Continent*, 1870). No
wonder the poet Elena Karina Byrne speaks of "an
AMPERSAND on a lack of sleep" (*Masque*, 2007).

Semanticists Ernest
Lepore and Kirk
Ludwig suggest using
"Bob" as a name for
an AMPERSAND
(*Donald Davidson's
Truth-Theoretic
Semantics*, 2007).

David Appelbaum refers to the "primordial AMPERSAND
of metaphor," noting that a figure of speech brings verbal
expressions and gestures to a "conjunctive point where
the measured and the unmeasurable are drawn ineluctably
together" (*Voice*, 1990).

The ampersand's position above the number
7 on the keyboard is hardly arbitrary. Marcus
Tullius Tiro's original ampersand looked like a 7.

"Not so easy if you don't know a serif from an ampersand."
—Andrew Taylor, *Caroline Minuscule*, 1983

The ampersand is out to conquer the world, at least according to journalist Duane Dudek. "You may believe that the AMPERSAND ranks with the asterisk as a topic of interest or controversy. But behind our backs and without permission or consensus—I didn't get to vote, did you?—the fancy-pants ampersand, or as it likes to be called, &, has, in many cases and without rhyme or reason, slowly replaced the rugged, beloved and serviceable three-letter word 'and' as the conjunction of choice." The reason? The grammatical economy it offers when space is at a premium (cell phones and computer messaging), its beauty on a page, its inherent informality, and its ability to highlight symmetry (when the text on either side of it is of equal weight). ("Sign of the Times," *Milwaukee Journal Sentinel*, Aug. 19, 2005.)

The ampersand has been likened to the mark of a conqueror who has reached a pinnacle and is surveying his dominion. Imagine a particular schoolboy who has learned to recite the alphabet, "calling out each letter by name, and with triumphant energy, AMPERSAND—as if he would say, I am conqueror—I have surveyed with the fresh eye of youth the entrance on the field of glory and fame—I have entered the chaparelle of literature and found my way to the clear way—the open space of uncultivated nature—have embarked on the boundless ocean of knowledge—have seen the temple of Fame and its goddess kindly and gently leading me by the hand—still pointing upward and onward to the interminable forests still to be surveyed by the eye of science—still to be embraced in the concentric circles of its advancement still to become the abode of other children who will radiate light from the illumined path of civilization and refinement" (Pat Murphy, "Ampersand," *The Opal*, 1854).

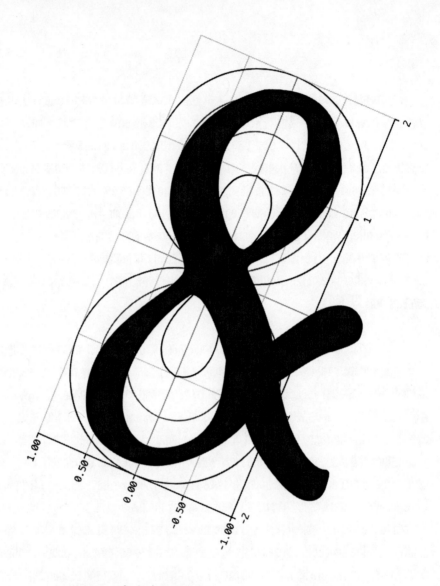

Cleverly it finds the sum,
By unifying parts & whole,
Combined in one continuum,
Of life & death, you & me,
This random moment & eternity.

———◆———Irene Smullyan Sloan, "The Ampersand,"
*Weeper, Laugh!,* 2005

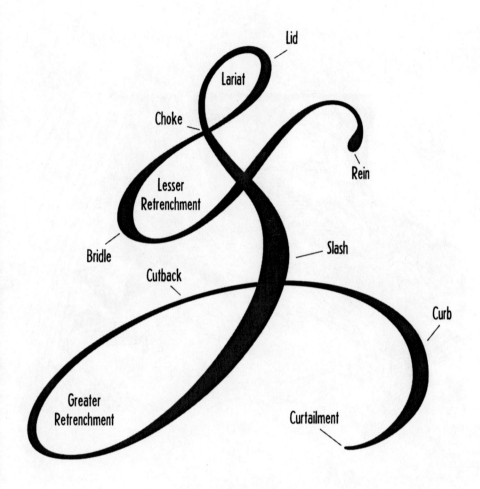

Lid

Lariat

Choke

Rein

Lesser
Retrenchment

Bridle

Slash

Cutback

Curb

Greater
Retrenchment

Curtailment

Lists are curtailed by an ampersand.

—Arthur Sherbo, *Studies in the Eighteenth Century English Novel*, 1969

Who occupies the quilt ———◆——— an ampersand in sleep.
———◆—Devin Johnston, "Pyramus & Thisbe," *Isn't It Romantic,* 2004

The first time you meet a royal ampersand on any given day,
use the highest applicable official address: "Your Majiscule."

The joining of our hands, the ampersand.

——◆——Peter Porter, *Possible Worlds*, 1989

# Ampersands Assess Relationships

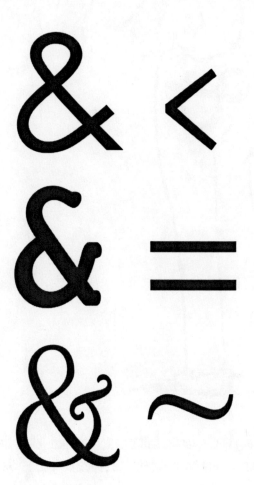

**INEQUALITY:**
The content on the left side of the & is lesser than that on the right side.

**EQUALITY:**
The content on the left side of the & is equal to that on the right side.

**SIMILARITY:**
The content on the left side of the & is comparable to that on the right side.

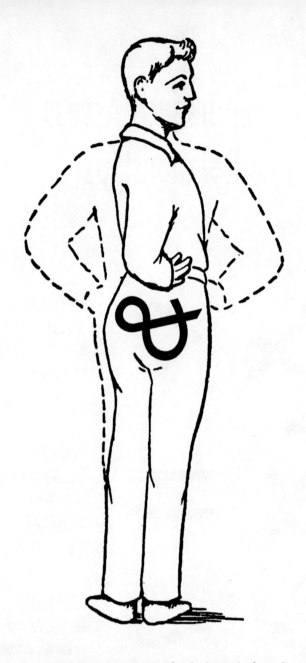

The curvaceous ampersand was a slang symbol for the buttocks from the mid-18th to the early 20th centuries. That's because in nursery-book alphabets it appeared "behind" the other letters (Jonathon Green, *Cassell's Dictionary of Slang*, 2005). For example, in the novel *Sam Slick in England* by Thomas Chandler Haliburton: "They had better let some folks alone, or some folks had better take care of some folks' ampersands that's all" (1844).

# The Dangling Ampersand

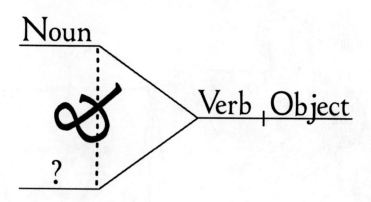

A "dangling ampersand"* tempts the reader to supply a missing word to establish syntactic balance. For example, in Walker Percy's novel *Lancelot* (1977), a character spies the following letters of a sign around a corner:

> Free &
> Ma
> B

"It is impossible to see more than that," Percy writes. "I have looked at that sign for a year. What does the sign say? Free & Easy Mac's Bowling? Free & Accepted Masons' Bar?"

Here's another description of the dangling ampersand: "Smith should not allow that ampersand to remain there, as if hinting at something it is afraid to say,—trembling upon the verge of it, and holding back without venturing upon it" (Benjamin Penhallow Shillaber, *Life and Sayings of Mrs. Partington, and Others of the Family,* 1858).

Often mistaken for a dangling ampersand is a dangling ellipsis, in which a sentence trails off prematurely, leaving you to stutter, "And? And?"

* John Edward Hardy, *The Fiction of Walker Percy,* 1987

Suddenly, I am somehow two personages in the law, deserving an ampersand, not a qualifying comma.

◆——Marla Brettschneider, *The Family Flamboyant*, 2006

An ampersand is symbolic of a fly-fishing hook,
according to the *All Men Scrapbook Pages* (2005).

Is there such a thing as a lowercase ampersand? Though unknown to modern writers, the ampersand of olden times appeared in both uppercase and lowercase forms.

The ampersand was the first ligature to win the game Twister.

Those with a fondness for beginning a sentence with an ampersand have a "kindred spirit" in the English poet Thomas Gray (1716-1771). "Kindred spirit" is one of Gray's poetic phrases that entered the English lexicon.

He had the Word,
had it from on high, while I,
previous to alphabets, superfluous as ampersand,
curled on chaos still my edges blurred.

———◆———Pamela Hadas, "The Passion of Lilith," 1980

Sea Ampersand

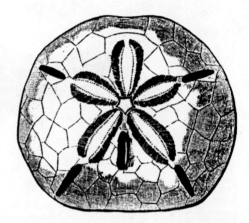

Sea Asterisk

On the beach an
ampersand
Surrounded by the sand

———————◆———Wintersox, *Here Comes
the Party People*, 2007

An ampersand "lying on its back and kicking its heels in the air" is found in the inscription of a 19th century church bell in England (Joyce Dodds, *Hertfordshire Bellfounders*, 2003).

The Emir of Ampersand.

————————Diana Wynne Jones,
*Year of the Griffin*, 2000

Lillith "looked at the table in front of her and saw an ampersand crack in the table's surface."

————◆————Josh Emmons, *The Loss of Leon Meed*, 2005

The English poet William Wordsworth not only dressed
to the nines, but he also shaped his ampersand like a 9
(Philip Gaskell, *The Book Collector*, 1955).

Cornelius Ampersand, in the satirical writings of Wolcott Gibbs, is a pioneer settler "along the thundering marge of Lake Prolix" (1947).

The ampersand is a figure eight, an hour-glass.
————◆————*The Centennial Review*, 1957

The ampersand is the only survivor of what was a great army.
———◆———Arundell Esdaile, *A Student's Manual of Bibliography*, 1931

Señora Etcetera & Lady Ampersand.

———•——— *The Cabellian: A Journal of the
Second American Renaissance*, 1969

Steamship Ampersand lost at sea ———◆——— April, 1878.
———◆———Jim Woodman, *The Book of Key Biscayne*, 1961

# A Nose for Ampersands

Poised like an ampersand at dawn, balanced on hunger's
nostril counting breaths ———◆———anapana.*

———◆——— "Nothing to Do," *New Poetry: Magazine of the
Poetry Society of Australia,* Vol. 23, 1975

\* Anapana is a mindful breathing practice of Buddhism.

ABCDEFGHIJKLMNOPQRSTUVWXYZ&

The ampersand has been provocatively deemed "the et cetera at the end of the alphabet," as if to suggest that a number of unknown letters might follow (M.A. Courtney, *Glossary of Words in Use in Cornwall*, 1880). In olden times, children learning to write their alphabets would always end with the ampersand.

# WH&T'S in a Nam&?

**abc-and**
—Francis Green, *West Wales Historical Records*, 1926

This variation, of Welsh origin, establishes the ampersand as coming at the end of the alphabet, an "and" after the "abc's."

**amberesand**
—Manchester City News, Dec. 31, 1881

This spelling is derived from the French name for Antwerp, *Anvers*, a presumed origin of the symbol.

**ambersand**
—Jack Grapes, *Onthebus*, 1989

"When the ambersand (&) is looped in a high degree, there will be a protective, loyal nature present." —Richard Dimsdale Stocker, *The Language of Handwriting: A Textbook of Graphology*, 1904

**amersand**
—Elizabeth Evans, *Ring Lardner*, 1979

"He uses the amersand, then the word *and*." —Elizabeth Evans, *Ring Lardner*, 1979

**amp**
—Clive Maxfield, *The Design Warrior's Guide to FPGAs*, 2004

This is a term from digital circuit theory (combinational logic).

"The '&' (ampersand) character is commonly referred to an an 'amp.'" —Clive Maxfield, *The Design Warrior's Guide to FPGAs*, 2004

**ampassy**
—James Hooper, *The Gentlemen's Magazine*, July 1892

This word is of Cornish origin.

"The whole lot from A to Ampassy." —Arthur Thomas Quiller-Couch, *Shining Ferry*, 1904

**ampassy-and**
—Charles Earle Funk, *Thereby Hangs a Tale*, 1950

This word has been traced back to the English town of Corringham, Essex.

**am-passy-and**
—John Stephen Farmer, *Slang and Its Analogues Past and Present*, 1903

This is a word from colloquial English slang.

**ampasty**
—Alfred Langdon Elwyn, *Glossary of Supposed Americanisms*, 1859

**ampazad**
—John Stephen Farmer, *Slang and Its Analogues Past and Present*, 1903

The "zad" at the end of this word recalls the "zed" or Z of the alphabet, traditionally followed by the ampersand (here shortened to "ampa").

This is a word from colloquial English slang.

**amper**
—*The New Hacker's Dictionary*, 1991

This word is a shorthand in the hacking community.

**ampers**
—Douglas Macmillan, *Word-lore*, 1928

"Ampers is a corruption of 'and per se.'" —Douglas Macmillan, *Word-lore*, 1928

**ampersamand**
—George Gibson Neill Wright, *The Writing of Arabic Numerals*, 1952

"Other generations may yet speak of an 'ampersand and,' and then of an 'ampersamand.'" —George Gibson Neill Wright, *The Writing of Arabic Numerals*, 1952

**ampers and**
—Douglas Macmillan, *Word-lore*, 1928

"All the way through the alphabet to Z and Ampers And." —Donald Davidson, *The Big Ballad Jamboree*, 1996

**amper's and**
—Harry Alfred Long, *Personal and Family Names*, 1883

"Lumping together X, Y, Z, and Amper's and." —Jessie Bedford, *English Children in the Olden Time*, 1907

**ampersand**

This spelling of the word dates back to the mid-19th century.

"Ampersand is an 'honorary' letter. It used to be the 27-th letter in the alphabet." —John Burkardt, "Wordplay," 2002

"It is one of the worst things about our detestable time that this ancient . . . thing 'ampersand' is forgotten." —Hilaire Belloc, *On*, 1923

"Is this end or ampersand?" —Norman MacCaig, *Collected Poems*, 1985

"I envy the hyphen, the ampersand, whatever bargain they've made for beauty." —Brenda Hillman, *Fortress: Poems*, 1989

**ampersand-and**
—George Gibson Neill Wright, *The Writing of Arabic Numerals*, 1952

"Other generations may yet speak of an 'ampersand-and,' and then of an 'ampersamand.'" —George Gibson Neill Wright, *The Writing of Arabic Numerals*, 1952

**ampersandwich**
—Bill D., *rexwordpuzzle.blogspot.com*

This is a crossword puzzles term, referring to an answer that contains a conjunction between two initials.

**amperstand**
—Anne Hemingway, *The Colour of Love*, 2004

"It was a beautiful gold ring with their initials, Y & L, in the center; instead of an amperstand, there was a small diamond." —Anne Hemingway, *The Colour of Love*, 2004

## ampersant

—Prof. Joynes, qtd. in *Studies and Notes in Philology and Literature*, Vol. 2, 1893

In this corruption of the word, the ending "ant" seems to ignore its origin as "and." Prof. Joynes recalls saying "ampersant" "without the slightest idea . . . that it contained any trace of the word *and*" (qtd. in *Studies and Notes in Philology and Literature*, Vol. 2, 1893).

## amperse-and

—Gilbert Milligan Tucker, *American English*, 1921

This spelling of *ampersand* appears in several Mother Goose rhymes. For example, "Z and amperse-and go to school at command" (*Mother Goose's Melodies for Children*, 1869).

"Amperse-and I'm sure will thoroughly understand." —Henry Morgan Hawkes, *Lays and Lyrics*, 1900

## amperzand

—James Hooper, *The Gentlemen's Magazine*, July 1892

"My nice little Amperzand / Never must into a word expand." —*Punch*, April 17, 1869

"Webster, moreover, advertises us that & is no letter—the goal of every breathless, whip-fearing, abcdarian's valorous strife, the high-sounding Amperzand, no letter! Mehercule!" —Sylvester Judd, *Margaret*, 1845

## amperze-and

—John Russell Bartlett, *Dictionary of Americanisms*, 1848

This variation has been traced to the English county of Hampshire (John Russell Bartlett, *Dictionary of Americanisms*, 1848).

## amperzed

—Gilbert Milligan Tucker, *American English*, 1921

The "zed" at the end of this word recalls the letter Z, traditionally followed by the ampersand (here shortened to "amper"). This is a word from colloquial American slang.

### ampezant
—*Studies and Notes in Philology and Literature*, Vol. 2, 1893

The "zant" at the end of this word recalls the letter Z, traditionally followed by the ampersand (here shortened to "ampe").

### ampleasant
—James Mitchell, *Significant Etymology; or, Roots, Stems, and Branches of the English Language*, 1908

In this pleasant-sounding variation, the ending "ant" seems to ignore its origin as "and."

### ample-se-and
—Wilfred Whitte, *Is It Good English?*, 1925

This is likely a Victorian-era contraction of "and by itself and," similar to *ableselfa* ("a by itself a") (*Studies and Notes in Philology and Literature*, Vol. 2, 1893).

"I have heard it called *ample-se-and*." —M.A. Lower, *Notes and Queries*, Sept. 7, 1850

### ampsam
—*Studies and Notes in Philology and Literature*, Vol. 2, 1893

This is a variation from Framingham, Massachusetts (*Studies and Notes in Philology and Literature*, Vol. 2, 1893).

### ampus
—James Hooper, *The Gentlemen's Magazine*, July 1892

This is a contraction of *ampusand*.

### ampusand
—James Hooper, *The Gentlemen's Magazine*, July 1892

"He thought it [the letter z] had only been put there to finish off th' alphabet like, though ampusand would ha' done as well." —George Eliot, *Adam Bede*, 1859

**ampus-and**
  —*The Cambridge Review*, 1882

The satirical periodical Punch invented a character called Mr. Ampus-Annd: "All Mr. Ampus-Annd will say when asked for his view is: 'You tell me'" (1936).

**ampus-end**
  —John Stephen Farmer, *Slang and Its Analogues Past and Present*, 1903

This is an example of colloquial English slang.

**ampussy**
  —James Hooper, *The Gentlemen's Magazine*, July 1892

The "pussy" has been likened to "a pussy-cat sitting up and raising its fore-paw!" (Edward Walford, *The Antiquary*, Vol. XXXII, 1896).

**am pussy am**
  —David Gibbs, Pentagram: The Compendium, 1993

**ampussy and**
  —John Stephen Farmer, *Slang and Its Analogues Past and Present*, 1903

"I also found 'ampussy and' — I hardly know how to write it — remembered beyond the ocean." —Edward Augustus Freeman, *Some Impressions of the United States*, 1883

**ampussy-and**
  —Charles Earle Funk, *Thereby Hangs a Tale*, 1950

**ampuzzand**
  —M.A. Lower, *Notes and Queries*, Sept. 7, 1850

**amsiam**
  —Charles Earle Funk, *Thereby Hangs a Tale*, 1950

This word is of Kentish dialect. "Amsiam: always thus called by children, and named after the letter Z when saying the alphabet." —Joseph Wright, *The English Dialect Dictionary*, 1970

**and-by-itself-and**
  —Aldred Ainger, *Notes and Queries*, Dec. 2, 1871

"Ride behind the sulky of And-by-itself-and." —Charles Lamb, *Mr. H.*, 1807

**and-parcy**
—*A Glossary of North Country Words*, 1829

This is an expression from Northern English dialect. It is a variation of *parcy-and*.

**andpassy**
—John Stephen Farmer, *Slang and Its Analogues Past and Present*, 1903

"'Andpassy' is the name that, as a boy, I used to hear given to this symbol." —Vincent Stuckey Lean, *Lean's Collectanea*, 1904

**andpersand**
—Bim Sherman, *The Century*, 1878

This spelling was suggested alongside *ampersand* in Gilbert Milligan Tucker's *American English*, 1921.

**and-pussey-and**
—*Miscellaneous Notes and Queries*, Vol. XII, 1894

**and-pussy-and**
—Abram Smythe Palmer, *The Folk and their Word-Lore*, 1904

"'And-pussy-and' because its shape (&) suggests a pussy-cat sitting up and raising its fore-paw!" —Edward Walford, *The Antiquary*, Vol. XXXII, 1896

**ann passy ann**
—John Stephen Farmer, *Slang and Its Analogues Past and Present*, 1903

This is a colloquial English expression.

**ann-pussy-ann**
—Edward Shippen, "Educational Antiques," *Pennsylvania School Journal*, Sept. 1874

The ampersand "was allowed by some teachers to pass under the name 'Ann-pussy-Ann,' as I am advised by an ancient lady who never knew any other name for the character." —Edward Shippen, "Educational Antiques," *Pennsylvania School Journal*, Sept. 1874

**anparse**
—Joseph Wright, *The English Dialect Dictionary*, 1961

This is a contraction of "and per se," from English slang.

**anparsil**
—Joseph Wright, *The English Dialect Dictionary*, 1961

This variation has been traced back to the dialect of Leeds, in northern England (C. Clough Robinson, *The Dialect of Leeds and Its Neighbourhood*, 1862).

**anparsy**
—Joseph Wright, *The English Dialect Dictionary*, 1961

This variation is an example of Yorkshire dialect (Marmaduke Charles Frederick Morris, *Yorkshire Folk-Talk*, 1892).

**anpassal**
—Samuel Dyer, *Dialect of the West Riding of Yorkshire*, 1891

This is a contraction of "and parcel," from Yorkshire dialect. "Anpassal is the finish of the alphabet, and means, I suppose, *and parcel*" (Samuel Dyer, *Dialect of the West Riding of Yorkshire*, 1891).

**anpasty**
—Joseph Wright, *The English Dialect Dictionary*, 1961

In the dialect of East Anglia, this word means "and past Y" (even though the ampersand technically comes after the letter Z) (Robert Forby, *The Vocabulary of East Anglia*, 1830.)

**an-pasty**
—James Mitchell's *Significant Etymology; or, Roots, Stems, and Branches of the English Language*, 1908

This is a variation of the East Anglican word meaning "and past Y."

**anpusan**
—Edward Shippen, "Educational Antiques," *Pennsylvania School Journal*, Sept. 1874

This is a "careless and hurried" pronunciation of ampersand (Edward Shippen, "Educational Antiques," *Pennsylvania School Journal*, Sept. 1874).

**anversand**
—*Manchester City News*, Dec. 31, 1881

This spelling presumes the ampersand's origin in the printing presses of Antwerp (*Anvers* in French).

**aperse-and**
—John Stephen Farmer, *Slang and Its Analogues Past and Present*, 1903

This is a contraction of "and per se and."

**apersey**
—James Hooper, *The Gentlemen's Magazine*, July 1892

This Scottish variant of *ampersand* also refers to a person of incomparable merit.

**apersie**
—James Hooper, *The Gentlemen's Magazine*, July 1892

This is a variant spelling of the Scottish *apersey*, referring to a person of incomparable merit as well as to an ampersand.

**appersi-and**
—John Ogilvie, *The Imperial Dictionary of the English Language*, 1883

**apples-and**
—M.A. Lower, *Notes and Queries*, Sept. 7, 1850

This corruption of the word *ampersand* suggests that comparing variations of the word is like comparing apples and oranges. It is likely a Victorian-era contraction of "and by itself and," similar to *ableselfa* ("a by itself a") (*Studies and Notes in Philology and Literature*, Vol. 2, 1893).

**dingus**
—*Time*, Jan. 18, 1932

This word is used when the speaker can't recall the word *ampersand*.

"I have lived a half-century without ever knowing that dingus—'&'—was called the ampersand!" —R. H. John, *Time*, Jan. 18, 1932

**do-jiggy**
—Karlen Evins, *I Didn't Know That*, 2007

Language expert Karlen Evins calls the ampersand a "do-jiggy" (*I Didn't Know That*, 2007). This epithet is perhaps kinder than "thingumabob" and certainly more precise than "whatchamacallit."

**doohickey**
—M. Loy, *humor.darkfriends.net*, Dec. 21, 2001

This word is a blending of *doodad* and *hickey* and is used when the speaker can't remember the word *ampersand*.

"I do so love the name of this doohickey. 'Ampersand.' Gives me a symbolistic lexiconical boner, it does." —M. Loy, *humor.darkfriends.net*, Dec. 21, 2001

**Emperor's hand**
—William Shepard Walsh, *Handy-book of Literary Curiosities*, 1892

"The sign & is said to be properly called Emperor's hand, from having been first invented by some imperial personage, but by whom deponent saith not." —William Shepard Walsh, *Handy-book of Literary Curiosities*, 1892

**empersi-and**
—John Stephen Farmer, *Slang and Its Analogues Past and Present*, 1903

"A shrivelled, cadaverous, neglected piece of deformity, i' the shape of an ezard or an empersi-and, or in short anything." —Charles Macklin, *The Man of the World*, qtd. in *A Dictionary of Slang*, Jargon & Cant by Albert Barrère, 1889

**emperzan**
—Pett Ridge, *In the Wars*, qtd. in *The Romance of Words by Ernest Weekley*, 1911

"Tommy knew all about the work. Knew every letter in it from A to Emperzan." —Pett Ridge, *In the Wars*, qtd. in *The Romance of Words by Ernest Weekley*, 1911

**empus-and**
—Joseph Wright, *The English Dialect Dictionary*, 1961

This colloquial English expression recalls the *Emperor's hand* variation.

**empuzad**
—M.A. Lower, *Notes and Queries*, Sept. 7, 1850

This corruption of *ampersand* is also noted in Wilfred Whitten's *Is it Good English?*, 1925.

**epershand**
—John Williams Clark, *Early English*, 1967

This is a Scottish equivalent of *ampersand* (*The Encyclopædia Britannica*, 1911).

**eppershand**
—*Studies and Notes in Philology and Literature*, Vol. 2, 1893

This is a variant spelling of the Scottish *epershand*.

**epse-and**
—Joseph Wright, *The English Dialect Dictionary*, 1961

This variation is from colloquial English.

**et-per-se**
—Douglas Macmillan, *Word-lore*, 1928

This expression recalls the Latin roots of the ampersand.

**et-per-se-and**
—*The Journal of American Folk-Lore*, 1894

Literally meaning "et by itself, and," this expression recalls the Latin roots of the ampersand.

**hampersand**
—Harry Alfred Long, *Personal and Family Names*, 1883

This is an "English rustic" variation of *ampersand*; it also means "empire's end" (Harry Alfred Long, *Personal and Family Names*, 1883).

**man per se**
—William Shakespeare, *Troilus and Cressida*, 1602

Like *apersey*, this expression refers to a person of incomparable merit.

**parcy-and**
—Joseph Wright, *The English Dialect Dictionary*, 1961

This is an expression from Northern English dialect. It is a variation of *and-parcy* (*A Glossary of North Country Words*, 1829).

**parseyand**
—Edward Peacock, *A Glossary of Words Used in the Wapentakes of Manley and Corringham*, 1877

From Northern English dialect, this is a variation of *and-parcy* (*A Glossary of North Country Words*, 1829).

**passy**
—Joseph Wright, *The English Dialect Dictionary*, 1961

This is a reduction of *passy-and*.

**passy-and**
—Joseph Wright, *The English Dialect Dictionary*, 1961

This is a variation of *andpassy*.

**percy-and**
—T. Baron Russell, *Current Americanisms*, 1897

This expression is from American dialect.

**perse**
—John Stephen Farmer, *Slang and Its Analogues Past and Present*, 1903

Meaning "standing by itself," this is a reduction of "and per se."

**round and**
—Alexander A. Stewart, *The Printer's Dictionary of Technical Terms*, 1912

In typesetting, the ampersand is "sometimes called the *round and*" (Alexander A. Stewart, *The Printer's Dictionary of Technical Terms*, 1912).

**semper and**
—William Holloway, *A General Dictionary of Provincialisms*, 1840

This colloquialism has been traced back to East Sussex, England.

**short and**
—Vincent Stuckey Lean, *Lean's Collectanea*, 1904

This variation, used by typesetters, acknowledges the ampersand symbol as being a short form of "and" (George Burnham Ives, *Text, Type and Style*, 1921).

**thingy**
—Robert J. Sawyer, *Rollback*, 2007

"Hey, there's that 'and' thingy again." —Robert J. Sawyer, *Rollback*, 2007

**typewriter and**
—Lawrence Weiner, *Bomb Magazine*, Winter 1996

"You really think there's a significance to the use of the ampersand which for years I called the 'typewriter and.' It's like the choice of saying 'They are not,' or 'They ain't.' They're both correct, but they both connote a different placement within society." —Lawrence Weiner, interviewed by Marjorie Welish, *Bomb Magazine*, Winter 1996

**zempy zed**
—James Mitchell, *Significant Etymology; or, Roots, Stems, and Branches of the English Language*, 1908

This variation celebrates the ampersand's alphabetical proximity to the letter Z.

**zumpy-zed**
—Abram Smythe Palmer, *Folk-Etymology*, 1882

This colloquialism draws attention to the ampersand's alphabetical proximity to the letter Z.

**zumzy-zan**
—John Stephen Farmer, *Slang and Its Analogues Past and Present*, 1903

This is a colloquial English expression.

Made in the USA